Practical Use of Psychic Powers

By
C. W. Leadbeater

Copyright © 2022 Lamp of Trismegistus. All rights reserved. No part of this publication may be reproduced or transmitted in any form or by any means, electronic or mechanical, including photocopying, recording, or by any information storage and retrieval system, without permission in writing from Lamp of Trismegistus. Reviewers may quote brief passages.

ISBN: 978-1-63118-603-5

Esoteric Classics

Other Books in this Series and Related Titles

Aurora of the Philosophers by Paracelsus (978-1-63118-507-6)

Rosicrucian Rules, Secret Signs, Codes and Symbols by various (978-1-63118-488-8)

On the Philadelphian Gold by Philochrysus & Philadelphus (978-1-63118-511-3)

Paracelsus, the Four Elements and Their Spirits by M P Hall (978-1-63118-400-0)

The Stone of the Philosophers by A E Waite (978-1-63118-509-0)

Clairvoyance and Psychic Abilities by A Besant &c (978-1-63118-403-1)

The Rosicrucian Chemical Marriage by Christian Rosenkreuz (978-1-63118-458-1)

The Alchemical Catechism of Paracelsus by Paracelsus (978-1-63118-513-7)

Alchemy in the Nineteenth Century by Helena P. Blavatsky (978-1-63118-446-8)

Rosicrucians and Speculative Masonry in the Seventeenth Century (978-1-63118-489-5)

Qabbalistic Teachings and the Tree of Life by M P Hall (978-1-63118-482-6)

The Sepher Yetzirah and the Qabalah by M P Hall (978-1-63118-481-9)

The Devil in Love by Jacques Cazotte (978–1–63118–499–4)

Fortune-Telling with Dice by Astra Cielo (978-1-63118-466-6)

History, Analysis and Secret Tradition of the Tarot by Hall &c (978-1-63118-445-1)

Crystal Vision Through Crystal Gazing by Frater Achad (978-1-63118-455-0)

The Golden Verses of Pythagoras: Five Translations (978-1-63118-479-6)

Arcane Formulas or Mental Alchemy by W W Atkinson (978-1-63118-459-8)

The Machinery of the Mind by Dion Fortune (978-1-63118-451-2)

The A E Waite Reader: A Selection of Occult Essays (978-1-63118-515-1)

The Leadbeater Reader: A Selection of Occult Essays (978-1-63118-483-3)

Audio versions are also available on Audible, Amazon and Apple

Other Books in this Series and Related Titles

Using White & Black Magic by C W Leadbeater (978-1-63118-602-8)

Jesus, the Last Great Initiate by Edouard Schure (978-1-63118-599-1)

Mysterious Wonders of Antiquity by Manly P Hall (978-1-63118-598-4)

Ancient Mysteries and Secret Societies by Manly P Hall (978–1–63118–597–7)

The Zodiac and Its Signs by Manly P Hall (978–1–63118–596–0)

Life and Teachings of Hermes Trismegistus by Manly P Hall (978–1–63118–595–3)

The Secrets of Doctor Taverner by Dion Fortune (978–1–63118–594–6)

Vegetarianism, Theosophy & Occultism by Leadbeater &c (978–1–63118–593–9)

Applied Theosophy by Henry S Olcott (978–1–63118–592–2)

Higher Consciousness by C W Leadbeater (978–1–63118–591–5)

Theories About Reincarnation and Spirits by H P Blavatsky (978–1–63118–590–8)

The Use and Power of Thought by C W Leadbeater (978–1–63118–589–2)

Commentary on the Pymander by G R S Mead (978–1–63118–588–5)

Hypnotism and Mesmerism by Annie Besant (978–1–63118–587–8)

Spirits of Various Kinds by Helena P Blavatsky (978–1–63118–586–1)

The Hidden Language of Symbolism by Annie Besant (978–1–63118–585–4)

Eastern Magic & Western Spiritualism by Henry S Olcott (978–1–63118–584–7)

Spiritual Progress and Practical Occultism by H P Blavatsky (978–1–63118–583–0)

Memory and Consciousness by Besant & Blavatsky (978–1–63118–582–3)

The Origin of Evil by Helena P Blavatsky (978–1–63118–581–6)

The Camp of Philosophy: Studies in Alchemy by Bloomfield (978–1–63118–580–9)

Audio versions are also available on Audible, Amazon and Apple

Table of Contents

Introduction...7

The Use and Abuse of Psychic Powers...9

The Trained and the Untrained...10

Studies Not Definitely Psychic...13

Mesmerism and Mind-Cure...17

Clairvoyance...19

Scandalous Misuse of It...21

Thought-Forms...26

The Work of the Thought-Form...28

Helpful Thought...30

Sensitiveness...33

Inharmonious Vibrations...36

INTRODUCTION

The word "esoteric" can be difficult to define. Esotericism in general can be seen less as a system of beliefs and more as a category, which encompasses numerous, different systems of beliefs. It's a bit of juxtaposition, since the word "esoteric" indicates something that few people know about, while the term itself broadly covers numerous philosophies, practices, areas of study and belief systems.

In a greater sense, Esotericism acts as a storehouse for secret knowledge, which is often considered ancient (by *tradition, if not by fact*), passed down from generation to generation, in private. At various times in history, simply possessing the knowledge of some of these subjects, was considered illegal and a jailable offence, if discovered. This usually included such general topics as Alchemy, Pharmacology, Qabalah, Hermeticism, Occultism, Ceremonial Magic, Astrology, Divination, Rosicrucianism and so on. Collectively, these areas of study were often referred to as the esoteric sciences.

Sometimes, the outer garment of a subject isn't esoteric, while what is hidden beneath it, is. As an example, Freemasonry isn't necessarily esoteric by nature (at *least not anymore*), but certain signs, passwords and handshakes given to the candidate during their initiation, are in fact, esoteric, in the sense that they are hidden from the general public.

Today, in the twenty-first century, such topics are readily available at bookstores across the country, and numerous main-steam publishers offer beginners guides and coffee-table volumes on many of these subjects, intended for mass appeal. Books like *"The Secret"* have turned previously arcane topics into household knowledge. All that being the case, however, it isn't to say that there still aren't buried secrets to uncover, ancient wisdom being ignored and forgotten mysteries to be explored. In fact, it is often that we are only able to further our own studies by standing on the shoulders of these disappearing giants.

Lamp of Trismegistus is doing its part to help preserve humanity's esoteric history by making some of these classics available to those students who are seeking to unearth the knowledge of these ancient colossi.

So, be sure to check other titles from our *Esoteric Classics* series, as well as our *Occult Fiction, Theosophical Classics, Foundations of Freemasonry Series, Supernatural Fiction, Paranormal Research Series, Studies in Buddhism* and our *Christian Apocrypha Series*. You can also download the audio versions of most of these titles from Amazon, Apple or Audible, for learning on the go.

PRACTICAL USE OF PSYCHIC POWERS

THE USE AND ABUSE OF PSYCHIC POWERS

Strictly speaking, psychic powers mean the powers of the soul, because this word psychic is derived from the Greek psyche, the soul. But in ordinary language this term is used rather to imply that we in Theosophy call the powers of the astral body, or even in many cases those pertaining to the etheric part of the physical body. To speak of persons as "psychic" generally means nothing more than that they are sensitive – that they sometimes see or hear more than the majority of people around them are as yet able to see or hear. Though it is of course true that this sight is a power of the soul, it is equally true that all the powers which we display in physical life are also powers of the soul, for our bodies, whether astral or physical, are after all only vehicles. What is commonly termed "psychic power" is then only a slight extension of the ordinary faculties; but the expression is also sometimes used to include other manifestations which are yet somewhat abnormal among men, such as mesmeric power, or the power of mind-cure. Since the will is the motive force both in mesmerism and in mind-cure, I presume that we can hardly object to the application of this term psychic power in these cases. Often telepathy and Psychometry are considered to come under the same head, although these in reality merely indicate a somewhat unusual sensitiveness to impressions from without. In truth, all of these powers of the soul are inherent in every son of man, though they are developed as yet only in a few, and are working only partially even with them, unless they have had the inestimable advantage of definite occult training.

THE TRAINED AND THE UNTRAINED

In my lectures upon clairvoyance I have often had to draw a distinction between the trained and the untrained man. Until we come to examine the matter practically we can have little idea what an enormous difference the definite training in the use of such powers makes to the capacity of the man. Practically all those of whom we commonly thing as psychic in this occidental country are entirely untrained. They are simply persons who possess a little of this higher faculty, which has been born in them as a consequence of some efforts which they have made to attain it in past lives – possibly as vestal virgins in ancient temples, or possibly as practitioners of less desirable forms of magic in mediaeval times. In most cases in this life they have used such powers somewhat blindly, or perhaps have made no conscious effort to use them at all, but have rather been satisfied to accept whatever impressions came to them. In India, and in other Oriental countries, these things have been scientifically studied for many centuries, so that there any one who shows signs of such development is instructed to either to repress its manifestations altogether, or else to put himself under the definite training of those who thoroughly understand the subject. The Indian mind approaches these problems from a totally different point of view. To the Hindu mere sensitiveness seems an undesirable quality, lest it should degenerate into mediumship a condition which he regards with the utmost horror. To him these powers of the soul are not in the slightest degree abnormal; he knows That they are inherent in every man, and so he is in no way surprised at their occasional manifestation. But he knows also that unless carefully trained and kept in control they are likely to mislead their possessor in the early days of his experience.

The Indian student knows what he is doing in regard to these matters, for they have all been classified thousands of years ago. There are many teachers in India who will take a man and train him psychically, just as here a man might be trained in athletics or in the practice of some science. In Eastern countries the whole thing is systematized, and all of those who are here called psychic and clairvoyant would be regarded in the East as somewhat unpromising pupils. Indeed I believe that many of the Oriental teachers would rather not undertake the development of a man who has already some small amount of these psychic powers, because it is found that such a man has usually much to unlearn, and is more difficult to manage and to train than one in whom as yet no such faculties have manifested themselves. In the East they have a thorough comprehension of all these things; with them a man is trained in the use of his faculties from the first, and the possibilities of error and miscalculation are clearly explained to him, and therefore he is naturally far less likely to fall a victim to them

In our Western countries clairvoyance has a bad reputation, by reason of the fact that there are many pretenders to its possession who are constantly unsuccessful and blundering in their efforts. There may be some of these who are barefaced impostors; but I imagine that the majority have really some partial development of this faculty, although they have often entirely misunderstood even the little that they have. Certainly no man in the East would ever come before the public, or be known in any way as a clairvoyant, until he had been trained far enough to be beyond all possibility of the ordinary gross errors which are so painfully common among so-called clairvoyants here. When we grasp this fact, we at once see how great is the difference between the trained and the untrained, and how little reliance is usually to be placed upon the latter.

Most psychics among us feel themselves to be infallible, and consider that the messages and impressions which reach them come always from the highest possible quarters; but the truth is that a little common-sense and study of the subject would show them that in this they are mistaken. No doubt it is to some extent gratifying to each one's subtle self-conceit to suppose that she has the exclusive power of communication with some great archangel; but if she will but take the trouble to read the literature of the subject it will soon become apparent that many hundreds of other people have also had their private archangels, and have nevertheless been frequently grossly mistaken. Of course no trained man could possibly fall into such an error as this; but then, as I have said, the vast majority of our psychics in Europe and America are entirely untrained. Some of them may receive a certain amount of guidance from dead people — "spirit guides," as they are called - but it is rarely of an exact and practical kind, and it usually tends much more towards mediumship and general sensitiveness than towards the gain of definite control and self-development.

I doubt whether any large number of our occidental psychics would for a moment submit themselves to the kind of training which the wiser teachers of the East consider necessary. There a man has to try persistently~ patiently, over and over again at the simplest feats until he succeeds in producing his results neatly and perfectly; he is expected to build up his knowledge of higher planes step by step from those with which he is already familiar, and he is not encouraged in lofty flights which take his feet away from the bedrock of ascertained fact. Our Western psychics would probably consider themselves much injured if they were made to work laboriously at self-control in the way which is always exacted as a matter of course in all Oriental schools of development of these psychic powers.

STUDIES NOT DEFINITELY PSYCHIC

I suppose that many people would include among psychic powers astrology, palmistry and phrenology. I think, however, that we are hardly justified in describing these as psychic, because in all of them the theory is that the results are obtained by deduction from matters of fact and of observation. The astrologer ascertains the position of the stars at any given moment, and from that he casts his horoscope or sets up his figure, and after that it is supposed to be a mere matter of calculation to discover what influences are at work. In the same way the palmist observes the lines of the hand and then gives his delineation according to the accepted rules of his science; and the same is done by the phrenologist from his examination of the varied configuration of the skull. In all these sciences the real proficiency lies in the capacity to balance the contradictory indications and to judge accurately between them; and many practitioners of these arts are no doubt aided in such decision by impressions which come much nearer to psychic faculty. To these last perhaps we might permit the name of psychic power, but hardly to the sciences themselves; so that I think we may put them on one side for the purpose of our lecture. It sometimes happens that one who practices these arts is in the habit of receiving impressions and communications from some astral entity — impressions which greatly assist him in judging accurately from the facts put before him. In this case obviously such success as he may attain is not in consequence of his own psychic powers, but of the additional discernment which ordinary astral faculty gives to his departed helper.

In the same way it does not seem to me that mediumship should be recognized among psychic powers, or indeed considered properly a power at all. The man who is a medium is not exercising power, but is on the contrary abdicating his rightful possession of control over his own organs or principles. It is essential for a medium that his principles should be readily separable. If he is a trance or writing medium, that means that any astral entity may easily take possession of his physical body and utilize either the hand or the vocal organs, so that he is simply one who can be promptly dispossessed by dead man. If, on the other hand, he is a materializing medium (whether the materializations are perfect and visible forms, or merely invisible hands which touch the sitters at the séance, or play musical instruments, or carry small objects about), the special quality which he possesses is that etheric or even physical matter can quickly and safely be withdrawn from his body and used for the various operations of the séance. In any or all of these cases it will be seen that the medium's part is to be passive and not active, so that he may be seized upon and obsessed without too great an effort on the part of the obsessing entity. It is evident that he cannot be described as possessing or using a power at all, but rather as able to assume a condition in which he can without difficulty yield himself to the power of others. Conscious Psychic Powers

It would seem then that we may reserve the title of "psychic" powers for the definite use of will or of the astral or etheric senses — that is to say, we may include genuine and controlled clairvoyance, mind-cure, mesmerism, telepathy, and psychnometry. A great deal of unconscious psychic power is also being constantly exercised, and of that I shall speak later; but we will take the conscious exercise of power first. This conscious exercise of these powers is only for the few among us at present. It is by no means uncommon to find men who have good deal of mesmeric capability; and a fair number of persons have considerable curative power along various lines; but still as compared to the total population these are only a few. The unconscious powers are possessed by all of us, and all of us are using them to greater or less extent,

To those who possess and employ these conscious psychic powers I would say that all of them may be used and all of them may be abused, so great care should be exercised with regard to them. There is a good general rule which is universally applicable with regard to all such matters, and that is the rule of perfect unselfishness. If those who have such powers are using them in any way for personal gain, whether it be of money or of influence, that is distinctly an abuse. These are truly powers of the soul; they are connected with the advancement of man and with his higher development, and it is for that higher development only that they should be employed. That is an important point for the person possessing them to bear in mind; it is the only safe rule that can be made for their use. These are in all cases glimpses of the future of the human race. If these higher powers which will one day come to every one of us are to be used by each man for himself, the future may well be dark and fearful. If, on the other hand, as they develop, men learn to use them for the uplifting and the helping of the race, that future will be a bright and a grand one. Our record tells us that in the remote past there was a mighty race which possessed these powers to the full; but that race as a whole used them wrongly, and in consequence that race disappeared. We of the fifth root-race must also in our turn pass through the same trial, we must inherit the same powers. Their occasional appearance among us now is an earnest of the time when they will presently become almost universal, when they will be fully understood and accepted.

The great question is whether, having followed our predecessors so far, we shall follow them to the end; whether when we have developed these powers as they did, we also shall abuse them as they did; for if we do, it is certain that we shall also follow them in their destruction. If, as may be hoped, we shall do somewhat better than they, if there shall be a larger proportion who will use these powers for the good of mankind as a whole, it may be that the doom can be averted, and that the common-sense and public feeling of the majority will condemn and curb their employment for selfish purposes. But if that is to be, if we are to have this larger proportion of those who understand and who use their powers intelligently, it is certain that we must begin now; now that these things are as yet only in seed among us we must begin by using them unselfishly, and we must put away altogether the idea of exploiting them for the sake of the lower self. There is already far too great a tendency in This direction; the grasping avarice of the ignorant leads them to employ every additional advantage which they think they can gain, in order that they may make a little more money, that they may obtain a little more advancement or a little more fame for the wretched personal self.

The dawn of these higher faculties must never be corrupted by such thoughts or such feelings as these. We must remember that higher powers involve higher responsibility, that the man who possesses them is already in a different position, because he is already coming within reach of grander possibilities in many directions. We understand this readily in other and more purely physical matters, and none of us would think of regarding the responsibility of the savage when he commits a murder or a robbery as in any way equal to our own if we should fall into the same crime. That is because we have a greater knowledge than he, and so every one instinctively realizes that more is to be expected from us. The same thing is true with regard to this additional knowledge — this knowledge that brings with it so much more of power; for added power means added opportunity, and therefore added responsibility.

MESMERISM AND MIND-CURE

In previous lectures I have already explained the Theosophical view with regard to mesmerism and mind-cure, so I need not now repeat myself with regard to these subjects. It is easy to see how the former might be misused — how it might be employed with great facility to dominate the mind of a person and to influence him unduly to favour the operator. One hears sometimes of such cases, in which a man desiring to obtain a position, of another one desiring to obtain money, exercises undue mesmeric influence and thereby gets himself appointed to some place which he is unfitted to fill, or perhaps succeeds in having money given to him or left to him as a legacy when it should by ordinary canons of justice have passed into other hands. It is common to see advertisements in the papers from men who profess to teach mesmeric influence avowedly with the intention that it shall be used in ordinary business, in order that the person who uses it may in this way get the better of the unfortunate man who comes into contact with him in the way of It is obvious that all these are very serious abuses; and I think that we must class 'with them that use of mesmeric power which is so frequently exhibited in public - that which makes the subject ridiculous in some one or other of many ways. On the other hand, there is no doubt that mesmerism may be usefully employed for curative purposes. As I explained in my lecture on that subject, it is usually possible to withdraw from a patient such pains as those of headache or toothache by means of a few passes, without putting him into a trance condition at all. Indeed I imagine that a large number of ills to which flesh is heir can be cured in this way without the use of trance. This latter should be used very sparingly, because it involves domination of one man's will by another; perhaps almost the only case in which it is justifiable is that of a surgical operation. We shall find accounts of its successful employment in such cases in the works of Dr. Esdaile of Calcutta and Dr. Elliotson of London. One may see equally readily how easy it would be to misuse the power of mind-cure. It is often employed as a means of making money; and it seems to me that wherever that is done there is a terrible danger of impurity in the motive and unscrupulousness in the practice. It is sometimes said that those who devote the whole of their time and strength to the curing of others must themselves obtain their livelihood in some way, and that in this respect mind-cure stands only on the same level as ordinary medicine. I do not feel myself able to agree with this latter contention. In the case of the ordinary doctor we all know that he passed through an expensive training in order to fit himself to deal with the especial needs of the human body; and we all realize what it is that we are buying from him — the services which his skill and experience enable him to place at our disposal. But the mind-curist is often entirely ignorant, and has undergone no preliminary training; in any case he is using a power which cannot be measured upon the physical plane, because it belongs to something higher and less material. If such a practitioner has no means of his own, and is devoting the whole of his time to the work of curing diseases, there can be no objection to his accepting any gift that a grateful patient may wish to make to him in recognition of the help which he has given; but it seems to me that to fix a definite charge for services of this nature is eminently undesirable and contrary to the whole spirit of occult teaching. This is a matter which every person must decide with his own conscience; but it is a dangerous thing to introduce any element of personal gain into the utilization of powers which belong to these higher levels. It is better to avoid in this case the very appearance of evil

CLAIRVOYANCE

All this is true also of clairvoyance. Any faculty of that nature which a person possesses may be used for good in a great may ways. For one who has this faculty higher worlds lie partially open, at any rate sometimes, and therefore this power may be used to learn. For this purpose it is necessary that the clairvoyant should make a careful study of the literature of the subject, in order that he may see what others possessing this faculty have previously learnt, that he may be guided by their experience, and may avoid the pitfalls into which some of them have fallen. A clairvoyant who does not study the subject, who makes no effort to verify his visions and to compare them with the experiences of others, is liable to be seriously deceived, and by his wild predictions and descriptions to bring the whole subject into discredit with those who do not yet understand it. But for one who uses this power with common-sense and without self-conceit, in a scientific spirit of investigation rather than with the hope of obtaining personal gain from it, it may be a source not only of great pleasure but also of great advancement. Not only may be obtain knowledge for himself — knowledge which he can pass on to his fellow-men — but by its means he may also learn to see when and how people need help, and to distinguish the way in which it can most successfully be given. By its means he can often see where a kind word is especially needed, where a loving, comforting, strengthening thought can be sent with the certainty of immediate result. The clairvoyant has at least a little more power for good than his fellows if he will only watch for opportunities for using it, if only he will think always of helping others rather than of gaining anything for himself. Beautiful possibilities open up before us when we think of the power that will be in the hands of all in the not-far-distant future; the man who is to some extent clairvoyant now is beginning even already to reap a little of the harvest of capacity for good which will come to us all as the race advances. The clairvoyant who is thoroughly unselfish, whose additional powers are carefully balanced by strong and robust common-sense, may do much good in the world, and may gain spiritual advancement for himself in the very act of helping his fellow-creatures.

It is not difficult to see that this is a power that may be misused. The additional information about others which it puts in the hands of its possessor may be employed, and unfortunately is sometimes employed, for personal gain, for the gratification of curiosity and even for the levying of blackmail. We see from this how essentially necessary it is that the clairvoyant should possess the characteristic of a gentleman, and when he belongs to the class which in Theosophy we call the first class *pitri* this is of course the case.

SCANDALOUS MISUSE OF IT

Unfortunately clairvoyance may be acquired by less developed souls who do not possess the instincts of the man of delicate feeling, as we may see by some of the disgraceful advertisements which so frequently appear in our papers. There we see persons shamelessly announcing that they are prepared to put clairvoyant power (such as it is) at any man's disposal in order to help him to obtain an unfair advantage over his fellows in some speculation, that they will help him to rob other men under the pretext of gambling or of betting on horse racing. In this way they are pandering to the lowest passions of man, they are descending from what should be a higher and purer realm into the foulest mud of the most degraded physical life.

Nor are these the only offenders, for we often see announcements from those who profess to teach clairvoyance or occult science of some sort in return for so many pounds or so many dollars. These unscrupulous practitioners are able to live and flourish only because the public is as yet ignorant of the true conditions of all such teaching. It is certain that no true occultist has ever yet taken money for occult teaching or information. The moment That a man advertises — the moment that he takes money for any service which professes to be of an occult nature — that moment he brands himself as having no true occultism to give. True teaching along these lines is to be obtained only from recognized schools of occultism existing under the guardianship of the great Brotherhood; and every pupil of these is forbidden to take money for the use of any psychic power. So all these people condemn themselves, and bear this condemnation on the very face of their announcements; and if they flourish and grow fat upon the property of Those whom they deceive, the sufferers have only themselves to thank for the results of their own foolish credulity. Once more I repeat that there is one, and only one, safe rule with regard to the use of all these higher faculties, and that is that. They shall never under any conditions be employed for any selfish or personal object.

Let us turn now from these powers which belong only to the few to those others which all of us possess and are using, even though we may be unconscious of them. The first and the greatest of these is the power of thought. Many a man has heard vaguely that thoughts are things, and yet the statement has not conveyed to him. Any real or definite meaning. When he is fortunate enough to have developed clairvoyance to the level of the mental plane, he will be able to bear testimony to the enormous importance of the truth which is expressed in that statement. If, utilizing the senses of the mental body, he looks out through them at the mental bodies of his fellows, he will see how thought manifests itself at that level and what results it produces. It is in the mental body or mind of man that thought first shows itself to clairvoyant vision as a vibration arising in the matter of that body. From the plates which I have published in Man visible and Invisible some idea may be gathered of the appearance of this mental body to the man who is able to see it; though the drawings given in that book are only an attempt to present in section and on the physical plane something of the far grander and wider impression which is really made on the sense at that higher level by the appearance of that body.

We man thinks while a clairvoyant is watching him, the latter will see that a vibration is set up in the mental body, and that this vibration produces two distinct results. Like all other vibrations, it tends to communicate itself to any surrounding matter which is capable of receiving it; and thus, since the atmosphere is filled with mental matter, which is readily set in motion in response to any such impulse, the first effect produced is that of a sort of ripple which spreads out through circumjacent space, exactly as when a stone is thrown into a pond ripples will be seen to radiate from that centre along the surface of the water. In this case the radiation is not in one plane but in all directions, like the radiations from the sun or from a lamp. It must be remembered that man exists in a great sea of mental matter, just as we here on the physical plane are living in the midst of the atmosphere, although we so rarely think of it. This thought-vibration, therefore, radiates out in all directions, becoming less powerful in proportion to the distance from its source. Again, like all other vibrations, this one tends to reproduce itself wherever opportunity is offered to it; and as each variety of thought is represented by its own rate of vibration, that fact means that whenever this wave strikes upon another mental body it will tend to provoke in it vibrations similar to those which gave it birth in the first place. That is to say, from the point of view of that other man whose mental body is touched by the wave, it tends to produce in his mind a thought identical with that which had previously arisen in the mind of The thinker.

The distance to which such a thought-wave penetrates, the strength and persistence with which it impinges upon the mental bodies of others, depend upon the strength and clearness of the original thought. The voice of a speaker sets in motion waves of sound in the air, which radiate from him in all directions, and convey his message to all those who are, as we say, within hearing; and the distance to which his voice can penetrate depends upon its strength and the clearness of his enunciation. In the same way the strong thought will carry further than the weak and undecided one; but clearness and definiteness are of even greater importance than strength. But just as the speaker's voice may fall upon heedless ears where men are already engaged in business or in pleasure, so may a strong wave of thought sweep past without affecting the mind of man if he is already deeply engrossed in some other line of thought. Large numbers of men, however, do not think definitely or strongly except when in the immediate prosecution of some business which demands their whole attention. Consequently there are always many minds within our reach which are likely to be considerable affected by the thoughts which impinge upon them; and we therefore are responsible for the thoughts which we send out and for the effects which they produce upon others.

This is a psychic power which we all possess, which we are constantly exercising; and yet how few of us ever think of it, or of the serious responsibility which it involves. Inevitably and without any effort of ours every thought which we allow to rest within our minds must be influencing the minds of others about us. Consider how frightful is the responsibility if this thought be an impure or an evil one, for we are then spreading moral contagion among our fellow men. Remember that thousands of people possess within them latent germs of evil — germs which may never blossom and bear fruit unless some force from without plays upon them and stirs them into activity. If you yield yourself to an impure or unholy thought, the vibration which you thus produce may be the factor which awakens a germ into activity and causes it to begin to grow; and so you may start some soul upon a downward career. Later it may blossom out into thoughts and words and deeds of evil, and these in their turn may injuriously affect thousands of other men even in the far-distant future. We see then how awful is the responsibility of a single evil thought. Harm is constantly done in this way, and though it is done unconsciously, a heavy responsibility lies upon the doer, for at least he knows that he ought to have purified his mind but has neglected to do so.

If it should ever happen to us to have a selfish or evil thought arising within us, let us hasten at once to send out a strong and vital thought of goodness and charity to follow hard upon the other vibration and, so far as may be, undo any evil which it may have done. Happily all this is true of good thought as well as of evil; and the man who realizes this may set himself to work to be a veritable sun, constantly radiating upon all his neighbours thoughts of love and calm and peace. This is a grand psychic power, and yet it is one that is within the reach of every human being — of the poorest as well as the wealthiest, of the little child as well as of the great sage. How clearly this consideration shows us the duty of controlling our thought and of keeping it always at the highest level which is possible for us!

THOUGHT-FORMS

That, however, is only of the results of thought. Our clairvoyant watching the genesis of this thought sees that it not only sets up this ever-radiating and divergent vibration, but that it also makes a definite form. All students of Theosophy are acquainted with the idea of the elemental essence — that strange half-intelligent life which surrounds us; they know how readily it responds to the influence of human thought, and how every impulse sent out from the mind-body of man immediately clothes itself in a temporary vehicle of this essence. Thus it becomes for the time being a kind of living creature, the thought-force being the soul and the elemental essence the body. There may be infinite variety in the colour and shape of such thought-forms — artificial elementals, as they are sometimes called. Each thought draws round it the matter which is appropriate for its expression and sets that matter into vibration in harmony with its own; thus the character of the thought decides its colour, and the study of its variations and combinations is an exceedingly interesting one. A list of these colours with their signification is given in the book which I have just mentioned, Man Visible and Invisible, and a number of coloured drawings of various types of such forms will be found in the companion volume Thought-Forms.

In many cases these thoughts are merely revolving clouds of the colour appropriate to the idea which gave them birth but in the case of a definite form, a clear-cut and often beautiful shape will be assumed. If the thought be intellectual and impersonal — for example if the thinker is attempting to solve a problem in algebra or geometry — then his thought-forms and waves of vibration will be confined to the mental plane. If, however, his thought be of a spiritual nature, if it be tinged with love and aspiration of deep unselfish feeling, then it will rise upwards from the mental plane and will borrow much of the splendour and glory of the buddhic levels above. In such a case its influence is most powerful, and every such thought is a mighty force for good which cannot but produce a decided effect upon all other mental bodies within reach, if they contain any quality at all capable of response.

If, on the other hand, the thought has in it something of self or of personal desire, at once its vibrations turn downward, and it draws round itself a body of astral matter in addition to its clothing of mental matter. Such a thought-form is capable of acting upon not only the minds but the astral bodies of other men - capable not only of arousing thought within them, but also stirring up their feelings. Here once more we see the terrible responsibility of sending forth a selfish thought, or one charged with low and evil magnetism. If any man about us has a weak spot within his nature - and who has not? -then this selfish thought of ours may find that weak spot and develop the germ of evil into poisonous flower and fruit. But good and loving thoughts and feelings will project their forms also, and will act upon other men just as strongly in their way as did the evil in the contrary direction; so that this opens before us a sphere of usefulness, when once our thoughts and feelings are thoroughly under the control of the higher self

THE WORK OF THE THOUGHT-FORM

It may be useful for us to think a little more closely of this thought-form, and to note its further adventures. Often a man's thought is definitely directed toward some one else; he sends forth from himself a thought of affection, of gratitude, or unfortunately it may sometimes be of envy or jealousy or of hatred, towards some one else. Such a thought will produce its radiations precisely as would any other; but the thought-form which it generates is imbued with definite intention, as it were, and as soon as it breaks away from the mental and astral bodies of the thinker it goes straight towards the person upon whom it is directed, and fastens itself upon him. It may be compared not inaptly to a Leyden jar, with its charge of electricity. If the man towards whom it is directed is at the moment in a passive condition, or if he has within him active vibrations of a character harmonious with its own, it will at once discharge itself upon him. Its effect will be to provoke a vibration similar to its own if none such already exists, or to intensify it if it is already to be found there. If the man's mind is so strongly occupied along some other lines that it is impossible for the vibration to find an entrance, the thought-form hovers about him waiting for an opportunity to discharge itself Unfortunately. However, at our present stage of evolution the majority of the thoughts of men are usually self-centred, even when not actively selfish. They are often heavily tinged by desire, and in such cases they at once descend into and clothe themselves with astral matter, and react strongly and persistently upon the man who set them in motion.

Many a man may be seen surrounded by a shell of thought-forms, all of them hovering closely about him and constantly reacting upon him. Their tendency in such a case is to reproduce themselves — that is to say, to stir up in him a repetition of the thoughts to which he has previously yielded himself. Many a man feels this pressure upon him from without — this constant suggestion of certain thoughts; and if the thoughts are evil he frequently thinks of them as tempting demons goading him into sin. Yet they are none the less entirely his own creation, and thus, as ever, man is his own tempter.

HELPFUL THOUGHT

Note, on the other hand, the happiness which this knowledge brings to us and the enormous power which it places in our hands. See how we can utilize this when we know (and who does not?) of someone who is in sorrow or in suffering. We may not be able to do anything for the man on the physical plane; there are often many reasons which prevent the giving of physical help, no matter how much we may desire to do our best. Circumstances often arise in which our physical presence may not be helpful to the man whom we wish to aid; his physical brain may be closed to our suggestions by prejudice or by religious bigotry. But his astral and mental bodies are more sensitive, more easily impressible; and it is always open to us to approach these by waves of helpful thought or of affectionate and soothing feeling. Remember that it is certain that the results must accrue; there is no possibility of failure in such an effort or endeavour to help, even though no obvious consequences may follow on the physical plan.

The law of the conservation of energy holds good at this level as it does in our terrestrial mechanics, and the energy we pour forth must reach its goal and must produce its effect. There can be no question that the image which we wish to put before our friend for his comfort or his help will reach him; whether it will present itself clearly to his mind when it arrives depends first upon the definiteness of outline which we have been able to give to it, and secondly upon his mental condition at the time. He may be so fully occupied with thoughts of his own trials and sufferings that there is little room for any new idea to insinuate itself, but in that case our thought simply bides its time, and when at last his attention is diverted, or exhaustion forces him to suspend the activity of his own train of thought, assuredly ours will slip in and will do its errand of mercy. The same thing is true at its different level of the strong feeling of affection and friendliness which we send out towards a person thus suffering; it may be that at the moment he is too much occupied with his own feelings, or perhaps too much excited to receive and accept any suggestion from without, but presently a time comes when the faithful thought-form can penetrate and discharge itself, and then our sympathy will produce its due result. There are so many cases where the best will in the world can do nothing on the physical plane; but there is no conceivable case in which either on the mental or the astral plane some relief cannot be given by steady concentrated loving thought.

The phenomena of mental cure show how powerful thought may be even on the physical plane, and since it acts so much more easily on the astral and the mental we may realize how tremendous a power is ours if we will but exercise it. Let us remember always to think of a person as we wish hint to be; the image we thus make of him will act powerfully upon him and tend to draw him gradually into harmony with itself. Let us fix our thoughts upon the good qualities of our friends, because in thinking of any quality we tend to strengthen its vibrations and therefore to intensify it. It can never be right to endeavour to dominate the thought and will of another, even though it may be for what seems a good end; but it is always right to hold up before a man a high ideal of himself, and to wish strongly that he may presently be enabled to attain it. In this way our steady train of thought will always act upon those whom we love; and we should remember that at the same time it is acting upon ourselves also, and we can utilize it to train thought-power within ourselves so that it will become ever stronger and more definite, If we know of certain defects or vices in a man's character, let us send to him strong thoughts of the contrary virtues, so that these may by degrees be built into his character.

Never under any circumstances should we dwell upon that which is evil in him, for in that case our thought would tend to intensify that evil.

That is the horrible wickedness of gossip and of scandal, for there we have a number of people fixing their thought upon the evil qualities of another, calling to that evil the attention of others who might otherwise not have observed it; and in this way, if the evil already exists, their folly increases it, and if, as is often the case, it does not exist, they are doing their best to produce it. When we reach a more enlightened state of society people will learn to focus their connected thought upon others for good instead of for evil; if a man suffers from the domination of a vice, they will endeavour to realize strongly the opposite virtue, and then send out waves of that thought toward him; they will think of his good points and try by concentrating attention upon them to strengthen him and help him through them; their criticism will be of that happy kind which grasps at a pearl as eagerly as our modem criticism pounces upon an imaginary flaw.

SENSITIVENESS

There is another psychic quality which all of us possess in some degree, and that is the quality of sensitiveness to impressions. We all receive these impressions at times. As yet they are imperfect and by no means always reliable, but nevertheless they may be noted and watched carefully, and used as training towards the development of a more perfect faculty. Many a time they may be useful to us in telling us where help is needed, where a loving thought or word is required. When we see a person we may sometimes feel radiating from him the influence of deep depression. If we remember the illustration in Man Visible and Invisible of the man who was under the influence of depression we shall recollect how he seemed shut in by it, almost as effectively as the miser was shut in by his prison house of self-centred thought. Those who recollect that impressive picture will at once see what it is that thought can do for this man. It can strengthen his vibrations and help him to break these prison-bars, to throw off their terrible weight and to release himself from the heavy cloud that surrounds him. If we receive the impression of depression from him, we may be sure that there is some reason for it, and that this is an opportunity for us. Since man is in truth a spark of the Divine, there must always be that within him which will respond to our calm loving thought, and so he may be reassured and helped. Let us try to put before him strongly the feeling that in spite of his personal sorrows and troubles the sun still shines above all, and there is still much for which he ought to be thankful, much that is good and beautiful in the world. Often we shall see the change that is produced, and this will encourage us to try again, for we shall lean that we are utilizing these psychic powers which we possess - first our sensitiveness in discovering what is wrong, and then our thought in order to help to put it right.

Yet this difficulty of sensitiveness also may be misused. A case in point would be if we allowed ourselves to be depressed, either by our own sorrows and sufferings, or by coming in contact with depression in others. The man who is sensitive will often meet with much that is unpleasant to him, especially if his lot is cast in a great city or in the midst of what is called modem civilization; yet he should remember that it is emphatically his duty to be happy, and to resist all thoughts of gloom or of despair, He should try his best to imitate on the higher planes the action on the physical plane of the sun which is so glorious a symbol of the Logos. Just as that pours out its light and life, so should he try to hold a steady calm serene centre through which the grace and the power from on high may be poured out upon his fellow man. In this way he may become in very truth a fellow-worker with Clod, for through him and through his reflection of it this divine grace and strength may affect many whom directly it could not reach.

The physical sun floods down its life and light upon us, yet there may easily be caverns or cellars into which that light cannot penetrate directly; but a mirror which is upon the earth and upon the level of the cavern or the cellar may so reflect these glorious rays that they may reach to the innermost extremity and dispel the gloom and darkness. Just so it sometimes happens that man may make himself into a mirror for the divine glory, and that through him it may manifest to those whose eyes would otherwise remain blind to its shining. Trouble and sorrow come at times to us all, but we must not selfishly yield ourselves to them, for if we do we shall inevitably endanger others; we shall radiate depression around us and intensify it among our friends. There is always enough sorrow and worry in the world; we must not therefore selfishly add to it by mourning over our own share of the trouble and the sorrow, but rather range ourselves on the side of God, who means man to be happy. Let us strive to throw off the depression from ourselves, so that we may radiate at least resignation and calmness, even if we cannot attain to the height of positive joyousness. Along this line also there is a great and splendid work for every one of us to do, and it lies close to our hands if we will but raise them to undertake it.

Another way in which it is possible for us to misuse this qualification of sensitiveness is to allow ourselves to be so repelled by the undesirable qualities which we sense in men whom we meet, that we are unable to help them when an opportunity is offered to us. Every good and pure person feels a strong sense of instinctive repulsion from that which is coarse and evil; and from this fact a good deal of misapprehension has arisen, If we meet someone coarse and vulgar we shall feel that sense of repulsion; but we must not therefore conclude that every time we feel it we have necessarily met with that which is terribly evil.

INHARMONIOUS VIBRATIONS

If we regard the matter simply from the material level, the reason for the strong repulsion between the high-minded man and the man whose thoughts and feelings are selfish is simply that their vibrations are discordant. Each of them has within his astral body something at least of the matter of all the levels of the astral plane; but they have used it very differently. The good man has persistently developed the finer type of vibrations which work most readily in the highest types of astral matter, whereas the man of selfish thought has scarcely utilized that part of his astral body at all, and has strengthened and intensified within himself such vibrations as belong especially to the grosser type of matter. Consequently when these two come together their vibrations are inharmonious and produce a strong sense of discord and discomfort. So they instinctively avoid one another, and it is only when the good man has learnt of his duty and his power to help that he feels it incumbent upon him to try, even though it be from a distance, to influence his inharmonious brother.

We have, however, to remember that two persons who are in every way equally good and equally developed may nevertheless be far from harmonious. Although the difference between them may not be so extreme as that which we have instances, it may nevertheless be sufficient to produce a sense of in harmony and therefore of repulsion. It is by no means safe to decide that, when we feel a distaste for the society of a certain person, that person is necessarily wicked. This mistake has so often been made by good and well-meaning people that it is worthwhile to emphasize this matter somewhat strongly. It is true that such a feeling when decided does indicate a degree of in harmony which makes it difficult to help that person along ordinary tines, just as when we feel at first sight a strong attraction to someone, we may take it as an indication that here is one to whom we can be useful, one who will readily absorb from us and learn from us. But nevertheless it is also possible for us to overcome the feeling of repulsion, and where there is no one else to give the needed help it of course becomes our duty to do so.

All, then, should try to realize these psychic powers which they already possess, and realizing them should determine to use them wisely and well. It is true that the responsibility is great, yet let us not shrink from them on that account. If many are unconsciously using these things for evil, all the more is it necessary that we who are beginning to understand a little should use them consciously and for good. Let us then welcome all such powers gladly, yet never forget to balance them with careful study and with sound common-sense. In that way we shall avoid all danger of misusing them; in that way we shall prepare ourselves to use other and greater powers as they come to us in the course of our evolution — to use them always for the furtherance of the great Divine Scheme and for the helping of our fellowman.

www.ingramcontent.com/pod-product-compliance
Lightning Source LLC
LaVergne TN
LVHW041503070426
835507LV00009B/782